W9-BJA-231

A Gift from the Heart

To: Sharon

From: Linda

This book is dedicated to my husband, Joseph,
and to the greatest gift we've ever received, our son,
Nicholas. Thanks to my precious grandma
Irene DeAngeles, Joni L., Hoori M., Maura F.,
Bob H., and to Seymour and Toe for all their
unwavering encouragement.

You Deserve A
Merry Christmas

Written and illustrated by Jenna DeAngeles

**Andrews McMeel
Publishing**

Kansas City

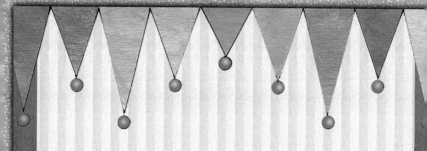

You Deserve a Merry Christmas

ISBN: 0-7407-3827-5

Library of Congress Control Number: 2003100784

03 04 05 06 07 WKT 10 9 8 7 6 5 4 3 2 1

You deserve a Merry Christmas because you treat every day with holiday style. Maybe it's because you are as sweet as home-baked cookies, as fun as opening presents, and you twinkle like Christmas lights. All right, you're also as outrageous as Christmas ornament earrings and you'll drop everything to hear a funny story . . . but you also deserve a perfect holiday because you're as good as hot chocolate on a cold morning. The season just comes to life when you're around. Yes, this is why you deserve a very Merry Christmas.

There's no time of year more suited to you
because you are unique,
because you send loads of Christmas cards,
because you cover the mantle with holly.

You make the season sparkle.
And when you pass on your joy,
you remind us, in all that you do,
of the true meaning of the season.

None of us has time to do
EVERYTHING we want to do
for all our friends during the holidays.
Precisely why I wish I were an elf.
If I were an elf, I'd make your
holiday perfect.

While you're out shopping,
I'd leave warm loaves of my
cranberry tangerine bread
in the kitchen.

If I were a Christmas elf, I would surprise you.
While you are out chasing down last-minute gifts
and sticking stamps on greeting cards,
I'd hang garlands made of pine limbs,
bayberry, and white bows over your mantle.

I would hang Christmas bulbs from your chandelier and tie satin ribbons on all your gifts.

I would try on all your Christmas stockings,
just for fun.

Yes, I would hide little angels
all around.

If I were an elf I would string twinkly
Christmas lights in all your trees.

I would do all this because you know
the real meaning of the holiday season.
Because you know that giving your attention
is more valuable than any trinket.

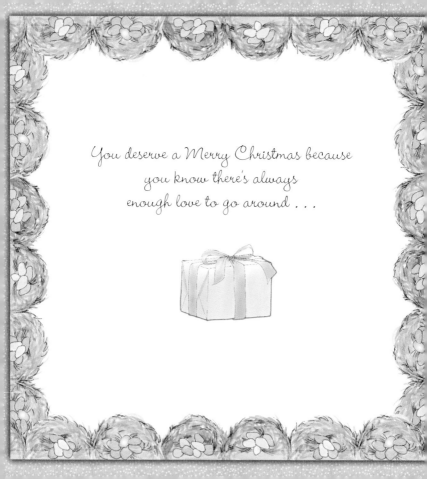

You deserve a Merry Christmas because
you know there's always
enough love to go around . . .

There's always enough love to go around.

because you treat people with kindness,
because you bring chocolates to the office,
because you always make Santa's "Nice" list . . .

because you have faith.

You deserve a Merry Christmas because
you know how to make a gingerbread house,
because you make your own tree decorations,
because you can be utterly silly.

Yes, you deserve a magical holiday because
you serve warm eggnog
to everyone after caroling.

You deserve a Merry Christmas
because you remember to give
everyone a little something . . .

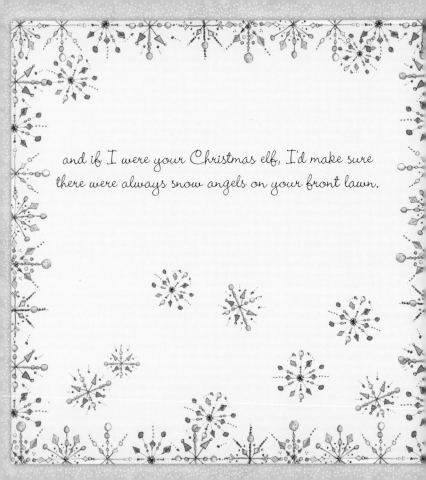

and if I were your Christmas elf, I'd make sure there were always snow angels on your front lawn.

I'd make sure the star was securely on
the top of the tree . . .

and the stockings were loaded with
all kinds of goodies.

All of this because you are special. You take time
to share the real importance of the season.
Because your favorite things of the season
are the smells of fresh-baked cookies,
the gathering of loved ones around a warm fire,
and knowing that the best gifts of all
always come as a surprise.

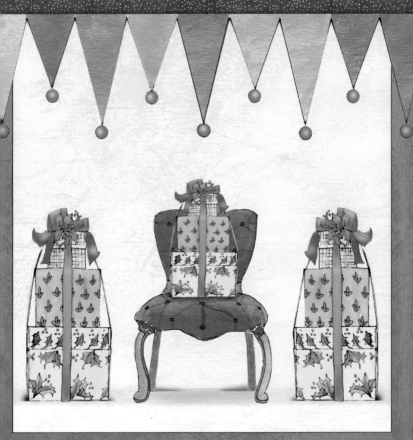

You deserve a Merry Christmas
because you'll drop everything
when your little one needs a hug.

You deserve a Merry Christmas because
you know how to have a swinging good time . . .

because you're never at a loss for words,
but you make every word count . . .

because you love all the old traditions,
but you're way ahead of your time.

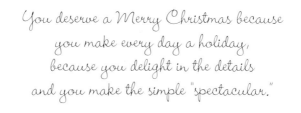

You deserve a Merry Christmas because
you make every day a holiday,
because you delight in the details
and you make the simple "spectacular."

You deserve a Merry Christmas
because you believe in the
magic of Santa Claus . . .

because your life is made of
love, joy, peace, faith, and praise.

Yes, you deserve a Merry Christmas because
you love your homeland,
because you buy vintage quilts, and
because you wear red snow boots.

You deserve a Merry Christmas
because you don't think snow . . .
you think snow globes!!!

Think Snow Globes Think Snow Globes
Think Snow Globes Think Snow Globes

Think Snow Globes

Think Snow Globes Think Snow Globes
Think Snow Globes Think Snow Globes

Yes, if I were a Christmas elf, I'd even wear one of those holiday sweaters (if you will).

You deserve a Merry Christmas
because you are one of the best blessings
of the season . . .

because you can turn the ordinary
into something extraordinary with one tiny ribbon . . .

because the wreath on your front door
is a welcome to all in goodness and light . . .

because you remind me that
I'm deserving of every wonderful thing.

The real gifts
of the seasons

children

Old Recipes

Traditions

vacations

Serenity

You deserve a Merry Christmas becau

Elfis Presley   Elfey Hepburn   Elfon John

'Twas the Night

're good at planning for the big event.

Elfa Fitzgerald   Elfizabeth Montgomery   Elfa Romeo

Before Christmas

You deserve a Merry Christmas
because your friendship is a precious
one-of-a kind gift.
Merry Christmas!

You have been blessed
since the day you were born,
from the moment you took your first breath.
When the angels blessed your arrival,
on your very first birthday,
it was decided . . .

you deserve a Merry Christmas
each and every year.